Why Me

The Medium

BALBOA PRESS
A DIVISION OF HAY HOUSE

Copyright © 2019 The Medium.

All rights reserved. No part of this book may be used or reproduced by any means, graphic, electronic, or mechanical, including photocopying, recording, taping or by any information storage retrieval system without the written permission of the author except in the case of brief quotations embodied in critical articles and reviews.

Balboa Press books may be ordered through booksellers or by contacting:

Balboa Press
A Division of Hay House
1663 Liberty Drive
Bloomington, IN 47403
www.balboapress.com
1 (877) 407-4847

Because of the dynamic nature of the Internet, any web addresses or links contained in this book may have changed since publication and may no longer be valid. The views expressed in this work are solely those of the author and do not necessarily reflect the views of the publisher, and the publisher hereby disclaims any responsibility for them.

The author of this book does not dispense medical advice or prescribe the use of any technique as a form of treatment for physical, emotional, or medical problems without the advice of a physician, either directly or indirectly. The intent of the author is only to offer information of a general nature to help you in your quest for emotional and spiritual well-being. In the event you use any of the information in this book for yourself, which is your constitutional right, the author and the publisher assume no responsibility for your actions.

Any people depicted in stock imagery provided by Getty Images are models, and such images are being used for illustrative purposes only Certain stock imagery © Getty Images.

Print information available on the last page.

ISBN: 978-1-9822-1675-7 (sc)
ISBN: 978-1-9822-1674-0 (e)

Balboa Press rev. date: 04/22/2019

Contents

Chapter 1
   New Life 1
Chapter 2
   The Terraced House 3
Chapter 3
   The Restaurant 5
Chapter 4
   Spilled Milk 7
Chapter 5
   Different Cultures 11
Chapter 6
   The Attack 15
Chapter 7
   Secondary School 19
Chapter 8
   That Man in the Van 23
Chapter 9
   Growing Up 27

Chapter 10
    The Meeting at the School..31

Chapter 11
    Almost taken 35

Chapter 12
    First Born 41

Chapter 13
    The Next Stage 45

Chapter 14
    My Hero 49

Chapter 15
    The Next Adventure 53

Chapter 16
    Absent Friends 61

Chapter 17
    Everything Is Taken 67

Chapter 18
    The Future 71

Chapter 19
    The Psychic Fair..75

Chapter 20
    Like a Duck to Water..81

Chapter 21
    Life as a Medium..87

Chapter 22
    Know Yourself...91

Chapter 23
    Older and Wiser..95

Chapter 1

New Life

It was a cold winter's day on Friday, March 12, 1965, but oddly, the sun was shining, as it subsequently did every March 12 thereafter for the next fifty years. I say *oddly* because, no matter what the weather had been doing the day before or was forecast to do the day after, the sun always shone on that day. On that day fifty-three years ago, I was born—the second child to a lady called Grace.

Grace was a South London girl, and her parents were of English and Irish descent. Her mother, Beth, my maternal grandmother, and her father, Henry, my grandfather, were unknown to me. Many years later, however, I felt their influence on me; they had passed on to me, beyond human comprehension, gifts they had possessed.

My father had arrived in London on a banana boat some ten years before my birth from Cyprus. His only possessions were his clothes and a small bag containing the crumbs of the bread and remains of the cheese he had packed for his journey together with a tiny pocket knife, a piece of cloth, and a notebook.

It was my parents' fate to meet at a funfair, my father catching my mother's blonde hair flowing in the wind as she laughed and screamed with joy while riding the Waltzer with some friends.

She was only sixteen, but within a few years, my parents were married. Their first child, my sister Sarah, was born in 1963.

Their divergent cultures were buried and lost while their lives grew and grew. They never even knew how different they were and what challenges lay ahead not only for them but for their daughter and two sons. I was the middle child.

When she gave birth to me, my mother told me, she felt that the experience was so right; it was as though everything was meant to be. Indeed, when she arrived at the hospital in labor, the midwife who would deliver me was a Turkish lady, which was unheard of in those days. My mother recalls how I arrived within minutes with no pain or pushing. Shocked, and relieved of her apprehension after she gave birth so easily, she held me in her arms and said, "He looks like a little college boy," because my hair was parted neatly. This was my first memory, looking at her face and hearing the tone and pitch of her voice, together with the love that radiated through me. The next six years of my life were to be the making of me and who I became as a man and am now today.

Chapter 2

The Terraced House

Taken back to a two-up, two-down terraced house in a London street, I was fussed over, fed, and gloated over to the point where I could have burst. My sister, however, looking out the corner of her eye as only a two-year-old can, stood thinking, *Who's this little so-and-so stamping on my parade?* She felt the first painful lesson of life—having to share. Unbeknownst to me at the time, she felt loneliness and almost an abandonment. My time for those lessons was yet to come.

That house was where I first saw spirits and where they talked with me.

I can remember my mother walking up and down late at night, waiting for my father to open the door after finishing work. He was working as a chef by night and a carpenter by day to provide for his family. On his arrival, she would run to the door, hug and welcome him, and then serve him his supper on an old metal, knee-level folding table, holding me in her arms as I watched. My father must have been exhausted by this time. However, seeing and being with this little family made his work and his purpose worthwhile. But deep down inside, frustration and rage were brewing. Little did I know I was to be his release and the excuse for his anger in years to come—I and I alone.

Three years passed quickly in that little terraced house, and it was during that time that my connection with spirits was forged and deepened nicely. I knew that somebody would be knocking at the door just before it happened and when the phone was just about to ring. I would also know who was visiting or telephoning before they identified themselves. I knew what my mother was going to say just before she said it.

These early years were happy times. Little did I know that the pattern of my life was fading. The good times were the calm before the storm, the brightness of sunshine before the darkness.

I know now that little house brought cohesion and happiness to those dwelling in it. If only I'd learned and known that, life could have been different through the chapters of my life, as the sun could have shone throughout. But with hindsight, I now know that, without my life's pattern, I wouldn't be here today, able to write this book, in turn enabling others to redirect their paths for the better. So, you see, nothing in life is in vain: nothing. There's always some good planned in adversity. You just have to believe, hang on for dear life at times, and know you'll come out the other end in a good place.

Chapter 3

The Restaurant

Henry, my dear grandfather, was a special man, a healer with his hands and a conduit for spirits, although he never discussed it directly. He often went to meditate in his study, watch the stars with his binoculars, or place his healing hands on a family member or a friend complaining of a headache or other pain. He was a generous man with his heart, his time, and his money, so he loaned my parents the money to purchase a lease on a restaurant with a two-bedroom flat above it. There was no bathroom, only an outside toilet on the first-level flat roof. But my parents saw it as the start of a business of their own, the next chapter in their life together. Little did they know it was the beginning of the demise of their relationship and the destruction of our family as they'd come to know it.

It was a white-table, silver-service restaurant, the old-school type with roast dinners, suet puddings, and real English dining at its best. During those next two years, my father started to realize I wasn't the normal kind of child, content and willing to comply with his likes and commands.

One Christmas, he dressed me up in a football kit, boots and all. Getting excited, he marched me over to the common to have a kick around, as he was such a football fanatic. He was not happy to hear me, as I stood rigid, say, "I hate football! Please, can we go home?"

That was the start of my private war with my father, and for the next eleven years or so, that's what it was—I would verbalize and he would smack. Well, at first he would smack, but it soon turned to holding and shaking, bending and squeezing, accompanied by his high-decibel screeching and the raging spit from his mouth as his eyes bulged, which shook me to my core. Soon I managed to learn what to say that would provoke his extreme loss of control. But I knew how far I could push him before he would inflict fear and pain on me that threatened to stop my tiny heart. I knew he'd never break my spirit, and even though I knew I should have kept silent, I knew my opinion was valid and would be heard. In any case, it was my life.

I found joyful times during the years there, riding the little yellow bicycle my beloved Aunt Maria had bought for my fifth birthday, one of only two bikes I ever owned. The other was an old, rusty granny's bike, which I rode when I was twelve. But I was grateful for them both.

I rode that little yellow bike all round London, and my parents didn't even know. It was during these bike rides that I'd talk to the spirits that rode with me, and they'd say, "Faster!" and "Further! Get lost in the streets!" And I did. They'd guide me home safely, so I began to have faith and trust and know I was never alone, even though those who stared at me saw me sitting alone and thought I was.

Chapter 4

Spilled Milk

It was while living at the flat above the restaurant that I convinced the milkman, Tim, to take me on his milk round. He agreed, and my payment would be a bottle of milk. It went well until one day when I decided to carry two bottles of milk to the doorstep instead of one. Being under five years old, I had tiny hands. That day, I slipped and fell, putting my hands out in front of me to soften my landing. The bottles smashed, slicing my tiny, soft palms quite badly. Tim quickly wrapped my hands in towels and rushed me back to my parents, who were just setting up at the restaurant. He begged them not to tell the folks at the dairy, fearing he'd lose his job. My first lesson! If someone has faith in you and gives you a chance and you fail, don't blame or betray him or her. Pick yourself up and try again.

Things seemed okay there at the restaurant and in our little apartment but they were not really. My mother and father started arguing; my father became more intolerant of everyone and everything. Then one day, he put my mother, my sister, and me into his white transit van in rather a rush. My mother turned to me and said, "When Mummy comes out of hospital, you'll have another brother or sister." She passed me a cap gun and my sister a dolly.

Mother returned home a week later with my brother, Robert. All seemed well, but it wasn't. Soon I noticed my mother wasn't the same; she sat staring at the floor, quiet and subdued, tears rolling down her face. Occasionally, she would talk to herself but to nobody else. The crying became worse; her gaunt, lost face was that of a woman troubled to the depths of her soul. My father would try talking to her, and he tried to carry on as normal, but to no avail. She didn't even show a glint of a smile or reaction.

I'd wake at night and go downstairs from the attic bedroom to find her sitting up alone smoking cigarettes. I'd see spirits sitting with her; however, she was as unresponsive to them as she was to our family members.

Grace had a gift. I know now that she was a medium herself and had dabbled with Ouija boards, only to have frightened herself and her friends. In those days, that sort of activity was associated with witchcraft, so she avoided any further discussion or practice. Little did she know that the feelings she had and the extreme openness didn't stop spirits coming through. This, coupled with my father's tighter suppression and restrictions on her, forced her to revert even more deeply into her inner self, blocking and shutting herself away. Finally, all the adults in her life felt that enough was enough; she needed professional help. So, with a diagnosis of postnatal depression, she entered a program for those with mental health issues.

I, in turn, was constantly being told the real issues by spirits. They told me about her regrets and her lack of self-esteem. They also explained the basic pressures of life's demands that were put on any parent trying to survive. Grace made it through life's challenges back then, as she does even today. She is a born survivor, one would say. Fortunately, my grandmother, Beth, lived close by so she was almost always around whisking me off to be with her at any opportunity. So, luckily, I had a substitute mother. I also had a substitute father, my spiritual grandfather Henry. The last year in that restaurant was interesting to say the least as so much happened in such a short time. I grew up fast and would never look back.

Chapter 5
Different Cultures

By the end of 1973, my mother's health had stabilized, and both my parents decided they wanted a building they could own themselves, so they purchased a small workman's café in North London with a four-bedroom flat behind and above it. It was run down and needed repair, but with my father's building and carpentry skills, that would not be a problem.

My mother picked our rooms and said I was to have the room at the top in the front as it overlooked a busy road, and I loved watching cars. Little did she know—but maybe she did—that it was the room in which, many years before, a man had committed suicide. Now I, an eight-year-old, a developing medium, was his roommate.

Well, a new life began—a new school, new London streets to walk, new dangers, new fears, and, of course, new friends to find. Each night I'd dread going to bed for fear of seeing the earthbound spirit that would hiss and snarl with disgust at my

The Medium

presence in "his" room and house. So I'd walk the London streets until as late as I could. I had yet to learn that my wanderings were giving me the best lessons of my life.

My older sister and my brother, who was only three, seemed so extraordinarily settled, as did my father. My mother, however, started showing signs of unease and distress again. It wasn't long before she was admitted to the local psychiatric hospital, drugged and sedated to the eyeballs.

I would arrive home from school every day, get on my bike, ride to the hospital, enter the security area, walk amongst the mentally ill. I'd always find my mother sitting in the same chair, staring at the same spot of dirt on the floor. I would talk to her gently, and she would not even blink. I'd sit for an hour or so with her. Then I'd kiss her cheek and ride the hour-long journey back home on my bike.

My relationship with my father was deteriorating rapidly. He would shout at the slightest thing, and only ever at me, never my brother or sister. I suppose he had to vent his pain and worry somehow, bless him. The spirits must have known I was able to survive anything he threw at me. These experiences were the making of me. Despite the pain, I wouldn't change a single part of my past.

As I watched my mother, I soon realized that she had lost her identity, but as the months rolled on and she started to find herself again, questions arose in my head. I was a mixed-race child of British and Turkish origin. I had been born between two cultures. Although my Turkish family, my father included, were not religious, their culture was very different from that of my mother's family. Father talked about "back home." He tracked my mother's every move, probably in fear of what actually happened some years later. He spoke Turkish to the Turkish family members, and I felt shut out. My mother and sister spoke to each other using a special slang, and I felt shut out of their conversation also.

So I couldn't refuse talking back to spirits. They were quite helpful. In fact, they would give me a heads up when my father was having a bad day. They would advise me to avoid him at any cost.

Family gatherings with my English relatives always included eggs and bacon if we were there for breakfast, and roast beef and Yorkshire pudding if we were there for lunch. At those gatherings I'd stand on a chair and entertain everybody by signing my Turkish songs. That was quite funny, the English family members thought, especially as my parents agreed when we children were very young that we would not be spoken to in Turkish as it could contaminate our English. Little did they know that those performances were my earliest presentations in trance. My father looked baffled at times because my Turkish words sounded strangely clear.

Family gatherings with my Turkish relatives were quite different. The women sat in one room, and the men sat in another. They usually ate separately, the men first, and then the women and children. The men would never cook or wash up. They would just be waited on hand and foot. But the Turkish ladies liked it that way because it was what they knew. Rarely would my aunties—my mother's sisters Carrie and Maria—join one of these occasions, however. They would have been like ducks out of water.

So, you see, I could function happily in both cultures. I had been brought up that way, and I knew no different. I did know that I was a child with a very sad mother, and I also couldn't quite grasp where I belonged. My mother, on the other hand, was English through and through. That is how she had been brought up. The differences between her cultural background and my father's were beginning to suppress her, making her feel trapped and caged. She tried so hard to be loyal and comply; however, that wasn't who she was or wanted to be.

Chapter 6

The Attack

As time went by, unease resonated through the family and our daily lives. My mother returned from hospital, continuing as an out-patient, and she soldiered on best she could, working at the counter, serving tea, taking the orders, and passing the small slips with table numbers back to my father so he could cook the orders.

I learned so much sitting and working in that little café. The customers were so diverse—builders, office executives, lawyers, tradesmen, even down-and-outs and drug addicts. As I served them their orders while I helped out most mornings, or while I sat and ate my breakfast before school, I'd listen to the different kinds of banter and interactions.

My mother would call me over at times and say, "If you're going to mingle in amongst the patrons, you are never to repeat what you hear, for if you do, you may be found lying face down in the gutter." That frightened me and made me nervous, but it also made me nosy and intrigued. What on earth would I possibly hear that could get me into such awful trouble?

I opted for the safer option, and that was to avoid anything that could compromise my safety; however, and ironically, the reality of personal harm to my person came home to roost.

In the vicinity of our house, vast numbers of council estate projects surrounded the small café my parents' home. My strange name raised eyebrows quite a bit among many of the neighborhood kids. On one particular occasion, I visited the local community center club after-school program.

I was greeted by two girls I had met there the previous week. With great concern, they advised me to leave immediately because, after my last visit, some boys— four brothers known to be local bullies—had quizzed others about my identity. When they heard my name, they had said awful things just because my name sounded strange. I must have been seen as an alien to that community. On hearing this, and after discarding my fake pretense to the girls that I wasn't scared, I went out the door at the first opportunity. I ran away and sat in a street far away because it was too early to return home. I was afraid of my father that day because he'd been particularly grouchy.

Every morning at 5:30 I would wake to the sounds of the milkman making deliveries and the sounds of cars driven by people who were rushing to work. I would go downstairs, have a cup of tea, and do various things to help my father prepare for the opening of the café at 7:00. I would peel potatoes, butter slices of bread from twenty to thirty loaves, grate cheese, and do other chores. On one particular day, my father was in a pleasant mood, so I told him about what had happened at the after-school program, and I asked him what he would do if he were in my predicament. He replied that it would have been different for him because he had five brothers when he was growing up "back home," as he used to call it. Together, the brothers were a force to be reckoned with, and other boys knew repercussions were always inevitable. My situation was very different. I had no older brothers or even friends to support me because the area was new to me. Also, these boys were near the top of the bullying pecking order.

My mother, as she did every morning, joined us at about 6:30 that morning. She was ready to start serving customers. I sat with her with a smile on my face, rather pleased she was home once again and not in hospital or constantly crying.

Soon it was time for me to start the three-mile walk to school. I remembered I'd left my homework in my bedroom, so I quickly ran upstairs to fetch it, only to hear a voice say, as I entered my room, "Walk the long way to school today." I was frightened, as I always was when I heard and saw the dark, opaque people. I decided not to take notice, and I quickly ran down the stairs, kissed my mother, and told her I loved her. I pushed through the crowd of men standing outside the front door waiting to get their hot tea, eggs, and bacon. I swiftly turned left—my usual route—and then turned left again up Beech Road.

I walked along that first mile of road and then walked the next mile uphill. At the top, I noticed a large young man walking toward me. I noticed that he suddenly increased his pace, and as he drew near enough for me to see his face clearly, there was just enough time for my brain to register he was a person I had seen at the community center the first time I had been there.

That's the last thing I can remember apart from being cold that day and wet as the sun had not yet risen, and the rain had turned the grim London pavement black. I usually looked down while walking—just minding my own business, only looking up periodically. The last time I looked up that morning, I heard an almighty bang and felt warm all over. Little did I know that the second-eldest brother of the four had used his signature leading right fist to knock me clean out. He followed through with a few kicks, amplified by his Dr. Marten boots with steel-toe caps and red laces. I lay lifeless on the street. What a cowardly act! I was just eleven years old, and a weedy kid at that. He, at the time, was approaching his twenties. Luckily, someone had watched the whole thing as he drove by; he probably even knew the thug involved. My rescuer waited for my attacker to depart and then

The Medium

kindly carried me back to the café. My mother, in tears, quickly rushed me to hospital. Her little college boy's face was badly shattered.

My mother insisted I should suffer immediate surgery to reconstruct my face even though I resisted out of fear. She assured me that, one day, I would thank her for this additional suffering, and she was right. I'm glad she made me go through with it, as I wasn't really an oil painting even before this act of pure unkindness.

Two weeks later, I was out of hospital and back walking that route. I was, at the same time, both defiant and nervous. I knew I had to face not only my fears, but the laughter and ridicule brought on by my appearance. My face was still swollen and bruised and monster like. The brothers never suffered any consequences of the attack because the streets of London ran under a code of silence even though it was so terribly cruel and wrong.

I was astonished by how my father, that great big aggressive man who had hit and terrified me my whole life, did nothing to my attacker. He didn't even mention revenge or express an outburst of anger against the perpetrator. Instead, he visited the brother's father to ask the reason for the attack, and he made me go with him. I stood in fear, but I was safe for the first time in my daddy's presence. My father was a large man, and even to this day has the largest hands of any man I have encountered.

The brother's father looked feebly small and drunk, quite pathetic actually. As my father quizzed him, he stood oblivious and offered an apology for his sons' behavior. Life teaches us lessons in strange ways. The knowledge that I had a daddy who could protect and love me during a brief encounter was worth the physical slaughter I had endured at the hands of that thug, and I was instilled, within a spilt second, with the feeling of love. I realized that revenge would only make me the same as the "thug brothers."

Chapter 7

Secondary School

I settled in quickly to my secondary school. I was at the top of my class in all subjects only because, during the last few years of primary school, my parents had sent me to a private school with financial aid from my grandmother and grandfather.

Those foundational two years created in me a yearning to learn. The teachers' approach to teaching was one of great understanding. I would love to have been there for three years, but the year in the middle was stolen from me because, without realizing what she was doing, my mother had fallen for the local Romeo, a man called Peter, renowned, I found out years later, for romancing and entertaining the hearts of vulnerable, bored, or lost—or in my mother's case, controlled and suppressed—housewives.

My mother found solace with this Englishman who was very much a London man, just like my grandfather Henry. He offered her a chance at freedom—a life in which she could love a man and still be who she could be. Little did she know—or maybe she did and didn't want to admit it—she was just a toy, like the others before her, during and after her brief affair.

My mother's lover had said she should leave my father and move up North so he could join her, so she, with a heart like that of a teenager in love, did as he suggested. She whisked us off within a week. I can distinctly remember my grandfather, Henry, saying to me on the day we left to live our new life, "Son, whatever you do, don't lose your accent." "I won't, Grandad," I promised, and I never did. And we went to live with my Auntie Carrie and her partner, they were school teachers who lived in Liverpool. I adored them very much.

That year was another time of learning as I encountered in a new school and a new council flat (after spending the first month living with my aunty).

After I just about settled in, that year flew by. During that time, my father visited us at the weekends. Soon Mother realized that Peter (the Romeo) had no intention of ever settling up there with us, so we returned to the café. My mother and father were going to try once more to mend their relationship.

Luckily, for my last year at primary school, I went back into private education. I got my head down and was completely happy. That last year was beautiful in every way. The headmistress and owner of the school was patriotic and loved monarchy. This blended with my English grandparents' love of the monarchy and helped me to feel that I belonged. I learned all aspects of etiquette and even had elocution lessons. I sang in the choir; in fact I was invited to sing a solo—"You'll Never Walk Alone"—on stage at the Christmas town hall celebrations.

That was the only year, up until then, that I had felt stable and secure. Little did I know, however, that my parents were like ducks on water. They looked calm and serene above the water's surface, but underneath they were kicking like mad. I believe they were holding on and trying for the sake of the children. Deep down inside, they were good people; they had just been brought up so differently. They were never going to have that happy ending. Tragic as it was, their breakup needed to happen for my brother, my sister, and I to exist.

The new day began at secondary school. I remember standing there, looking up at the Victorian building. There were thousands of boys milling about in the playground, as it was a all-boys school. I stood in my stiff, heavy, black uniform, thinking as I watched older boys playing cards, kicking balls, and chasing one another. I even saw a vicious fight break out. The teachers watched the combatants from the windows, allowing pecking orders to be established. As the fight finished, they walked out as a token show of presence while those involved scarpered. *If I can survive this*, I thought, *I can survive anything.*

I was put into the top groups on all subjects except football, of course. For the first year I hit the grades. In the second year however, things changed radically. The façade my parents were putting on started to show signs of leakage, and that, coupled with the fact that I was entering puberty ... well, let's just say I had the excuse be lazy with my brain. My psychic predictions were getting stronger, and I was seeing and hearing spirits more frequently.

Chapter 8

That Man in the Van

I had always had a paid job in some way, apart from working in the café. I had worked in a hardware store, a Turkish supermarket, a pie-and-mash shop, and even the scrap yard around the corner.

It was a situation that occurred the scrap yard that made me realize I must have been protected and looked after by my dear mother. On one particular day, I was working there as usual when a van drove in. I'd never seen it before. After he tipped his cast iron from his van, he drove the van onto the weigh bridge to find out how much he was to be paid. He began chatting to me, quizzing, probing—I realize now—about my interests and likes.

I told him I was working in the scrap yard during the summer holidays in order to save money to purchase a fishing rod and reel. He soon became excited and said I should meet him in the café around the corner, which he had noticed on his way to the yard. He said we should meet straight away, but I should wait for about ten minutes and then join him there. He advised me

The Medium

that he had a fishing rod he could let me have immediately. I didn't tell him it was my parents' café. I followed instructions as a vulnerable young boy would, excited at the prospect of immediately receiving a fishing rod.

Looking back, I remember sitting in the café with this man. My parents were so busy they were oblivious to my presence among the patrons. As I talked with the man, I realized that his eyes were strange. His face seemed rather cold, but his eyes were enticing, inviting, and convincing.

He finished his sandwich in about five minutes, and he said, "Right. I'm going to leave. Give me ten minutes and then come and meet me in my van. I'll take you to my house and give the rod. Don't worry," he said, "you can pay me at the end of the summer holiday when you have earned all your money." "Okay," I said in haste. I was excited at the imminent acquisition of the critical tool I needed for my next hobby.

When I arrived at his van ten minutes later, I felt cold but excited. He just sat there, staring straight ahead. "Wait," he said. "Wait. I'm thinking." At the time, I had no idea that a dear old man called Mitch Scrap, who worked at the scrap yard, had seen me get into the van. He had quickly run around to the café to inform my parents I had just got into the van of a man who had just been released from prison. He told them that all the people who worked at the yard were frightened of him. The man had just finished serving twenty years for the abduction and killing of a small boy.

I pestered the man to get going because I had to get back to work. But just as he started the engine, I heard my mother shout from the corner, "Get out that van! Get out that van now!" "Who's that woman?" he asked in a somber voice. "Oh, no! That's my mum," I said. He paused, and with a sick grin on his face, he turned to me. His eyes blurred, and he said, "This is the luckiest day of your life, sonny. You'd better get going."

As I ran to my mother, she grabbed me by the scruff of my neck and said, "You'd better go and thank Mitch Scrap. He may have just saved your life, you foolish boy." We never saw that man again, which was just as well because, after I explained everything that had happened, the three brothers who owned the scrap yard set up a plan for him if he ever returned, and I don't think it was money for scrap iron.

This had been another valuable lesson for me as a young developing medium. I had put myself in grave danger as my spirit guidance would be blocked if it was involved with thinking in my own head as I mulled over what had happened that day. I should never allow my thinkings to interfere with my intuition. And that made me think of other times when I could have been in danger or left myself vulnerable. *Maybe that man,* I thought, *who used to try and beckon to my friends and me as we walked home from the private school down Dawlish Place, was dangerous?* But he had seemed so nice. He had even offered me cake one day when I was alone and without any friends. It wasn't until I was about eighteen or nineteen that his face appeared on the news one day. Ian Holdness. My goodness. I thought, *Why me? Why put me so close to harm's way?*

Chapter 9

Growing Up

As I was slowly turning in to a man, I became more dismissive of my spirituality. By this time, my parents had had enough of the strange happenings in our home and my constant worry of never wanting to be alone in my room. Enough was enough. After some research, and on a recommendation, mother arranged for an exorcism to be carried out. The house would be cleared.

After the exorcism was finished, the priests sat me down and asked me exactly who I saw and what the entity said to me. Being a clever dick, as I then was, I said, "What did *you* see?" To my astonishment, they described my roommate to a T, even where he sat and what he had said to me. This was information I hadn't shared with a single soul. After I described other people I had seen, they showed me a book in which there were pictures of archangels. Some looked familiar to me, but I never really took it all seriously. Blessing me with their love, they left.

Soon afterward, my mother sat me down and said, "Son, you are a special boy. You may be a huge success in your life or you may turn out to be a bum. I don't know. But from today, promise me you will never mention seeing or talking to spirits ever again, for if you do, you'll end up in a mental hospital like me." I promised Mum I wouldn't, as I saw the sadness in her eyes, just as it had been when I used to visit her in hospital.

Summer that year ended quickly, probably because on weekdays I worked and on the weekends I'd go to the cinema or to Suzie's School of Dancing with my new-found friend, a lovely girl named Lorraine who lived around the corner. I remember her kissing me on the cheek outside the cinema and saying, "You're my boyfriend now." I should have realized at that early age that women are always in charge, but stupidly I didn't.

By the time I was back at school, I was growing hair in places that made me itchy. I felt lost. There was nobody to ask why and how I was turning into a monkey, or why my attention span was dwindling. My behavior annoyed the hard-nosed, disciplined teachers who stood for no nonsense. I began to dislike school even though my mother had written to British Airways for information on how to become a pilot, because that's what I'd always talked about doing. When the information arrived, my father said, "Ah, rubbish! You'll never be a pilot. You're not clever enough, you big ape." I scratched appropriately as he spoke.

By acquiring the information, my mother believed she was giving me a goal and an incentive. And she was probably right. The problem was that the teachers' patience was running out with me fast. Those masterful teachers quickly started to think I couldn't be taught, and they were probably right. I didn't respond to their aggression and threats because I'd been preconditioned to rebel against that sort attitude. That's how I survived my father. I was probably obnoxious and arrogant. I was starting to get so lost in my own selfishness. I stopped listening, as a young boys do who think they know best.

Soon the teachers didn't care if I attended class or not, and neither did I, come to that. My sister, however, and my brother were flourishing through school and life. They seemed so relaxed and happy. Why was I this oddball, black sheep? I was happy to sit alone and not worry about my future or my fate. I was happy to talk to the spirits others couldn't see, but now I could never talk about them to anybody because I'd promised my mother I wouldn't.

Looking back, I see that my life was so beautiful. I know now that my fate and destiny had been preplanned, forged, and set. Why did I have so many periods of worry in my life? Probably because I knew things deep down inside, and a lot of experiences were ahead of me.

My next job was one of great joy. I worked in a fishing tackle shop just down to street every day after school and on Saturdays. I made nice friends quickly. It was interesting that I made friends more easily with adults than I did with children. I was invited to adult parties and gatherings. Breaking my promise of my mother, I would speak and share my mediumship ability during these gatherings. I think I needed to do that to keep the adults' interest in me.

I was now thirteen years old. A very nice man named Simon said, "You don't like school, do you? I saw you standing in the street a few days last week when you should have been attending school." I told him he was right. As I'd me his wife, May, and attend a few social events with them both, I felt I could trust him. He offered me a job as a helper in his house renovator and decorator business. I agreed. We planned that I would take two days off from school a week—at first naughtily—and work with him.

Mother wasn't getting any happier. I heard my parents arguing late into the night with quite a lot of shouting. Although my father never laid a finger on my mother, his words must have been quite intimidating for her.

Finally, after so much trying, things at home were worse. Mother was back working in the café. Peter returned and was always lurking around, torturing my mother, who now believed she loved him. He played her love so cruelly without regard for anyone else it might affect. This situation taught me another lesson—never ever, bother a female if she has a partner. Ever. No matter how much you desire her.

Chapter 10

The Meeting at the School

As the months rolled on, I skipped school more often. I was approaching my fourteenth birthday, and the school had a legal obligation to make sure I was attending. They contacted my parents, and before I knew it, I was in a program for truant boys.

Looking back, I see that I was being selfish, putting my dear mother through further worry. After I had various private meetings with truant officers, they insisted the whole family come to a meeting because the problem with me possibly involved them. So, one Tuesday afternoon, we all set off for a meeting at their offices.

My father, mother, sister and brother all sat there looking at me as if I was a weirdo—until the lady leading the meeting asked their view one at a time.

The Medium

I was last and said—I don't know why, but it just came out—"The reason I don't like school is that the kids bully me just like my dad does."

This provoked the lady to ask questions of father. As I looked on, the rage in my father's face became more apparent as he tried to compose himself. I thought this was my chance—a chance for an outsider to witness his temper. "What do you say?" she asked me, so I goaded and pushed and pushed. It was the first time in my life I thought I could speak out publicly without being thumped ... well not immediately anyway, although I knew what would occur once we got home.

As his temper accelerated and my mouth kept on running, the lady tried to speak, but it was too late. My father flew off the chair and over the small table at me. He was like a man possessed. Something had happened as we all sat in that intimate circle. It was as though my father froze just before he got to me, his hands stretched out. Everybody else was frozen in shock because they didn't know what was about to happen. It was bizarre, like nothing I had ever experience before because, when he used to go for me before, my mother or sister would smother me to protect me. They knew he would never lay a hand on them.

As the lady calmed everybody down and repositioned the chairs and table that had gone over in the ruckus, I felt terrible. Oddly, I felt bad for my father because I could see the embarrassment on his face. He was the proudest man I ever knew, even though he carried that pride to his detriment. The lady said, "Why did you lose control?" My mother piped up quickly. "He was goaded! Can't you see that?" "Yes," replied the lady, "however, you are an adult and he is a child. You must control yourself no matter what." As the lady drew the meeting to an end, little did I know that, in creating that scenario, I had sealed my fate. In the lady's mind, she knew, and after witnessing this loss of control, she was in no doubt that I should, for my own safety, be removed from my family as soon as possible.

That was the last thing I wanted. As we walked to the car, I apologized to all my family members, including my father.

Why Me

My sister and brother were not too happy about having had to attend. They believed that I was the problem, not them. And my mother looked at me with such worry in her eyes that something switched in me, and I thought, *I need to change!* I didn't have a clue as to how or what my fate would be, but I knew for the first time in my life that the only person who could make me and those around me happy was me, and me alone.

Chapter 11

Almost taken

The night after that fateful meeting, strangely, my father was extraordinarily subservient. He didn't say a single word to me, and from that day, he never ever went for me again.
The next day, I attended school, worried about my fate. When I got home, my mother sat me down and said she had received a call from the lady at the school, and she had made an appointment for me to begin a trial stay at a care home rehab center for disruptive boys. I was to go there to check in on Friday. My mother had tears in her eyes because she so wanted me to settle and be happy. I think her medium gift was telling her this wasn't for me and other plans would materialize.

The night before my appointment, I was terrified. There were so many thoughts in my mind. I'd heard about these kinds of places, and they didn't sound like places for a weedy little foreign-named boy like me.

I sat in the backseat of the car on the journey to the center. As we came to a stop at the entrance, I said in my head, *You won't be staying here*. Simultaneously, my mother said the same thing out loud.

We walked inside. Well, it was awful. The boys were staring at me. Many were decorated by tattoos, self-inflicted with Indian ink. One even said, right in front of my parents, "Looks like we gonna have some fun with you!" We were then greeted by a rather large lady. She shooed the boys away and said, "We have been expecting you."

My mother looked at me, and I looked at her. She said to the lady, "Can he have one more chance? If he attends school, can I take him home?" "Oh, no," the lady said. "We've got him booked in now. It's not that bad here." Turning away from her, my mother whispered to me, "You're not staying here." Just then, she looked up and saw a boy who obviously had phycological problems.

Then, an almighty feeling of overwhelm came over me. It was a feeling of love, and I saw the man who had been removed from my bedroom. He said, "Speak! Speak up quickly! Now is your only chance!" So I looked at that lady and said, "I've been unwell as a boy, I have asthma and have forgotten my inhaler and my eczema cream. Without those medications, I could get very sick. I can't stay here without them." With a worried face, the lady said, "Oh, no. We can't have children here who have medical conditions like that. That wasn't in the report I received." My mother substantiated what I had said, and with that, the lady said, "You'd better go home. Other arrangements will have to be made."

With reflection, I understand that, throughout my life, it was very apparent that I lived each day, each year with uncertainty. Yes, plans were made in my mind; however, what materialized during the journey to each destination was totally bizarre to say the least, and in saying that, and no matter what challenges occurred, I always seemed to arrive at where I'd planned to be or acquire what I'd planned to acquire, even though at times I'd almost given up because sometimes the challenges seemed too much and I'd lose sight of my goal.

So, I suppose the message must be this: as long as you set your mind at something in the beginning, and are true to your heart, even if you don't have a clue how or if it will materialize, as long as it doesn't violate other souls on their paths, all will come true. Never give up, never give in, and accept that your journey may be tough and even change you along the way. I also realized that time would speed up or subsequently slow down in order to accommodate the pace in which I was to be taught a lesson.

I survived it all. Now I was sure I hadn't been born to be a victim of life's trials and tribulations. When I returned to school, it became quite obvious to me that the teachers had done with me and believed I was a lost cause. In any case, I had fallen so far behind with my coursework that catching up in a few months was nearly impossible.

As I think back now, I realize that what I must have been putting my dear mother—bless her—through was awful. She was steadily living through the hell at the café. My sister was flourishing as always as was my little brother. But Grace was determined to see me get a start in life.

My work skills were vast and varied because I'd worked in many jobs, but I had no real specialized skill. What I didn't know was my that mother had been assessing my situation and opportunities. She began advising me on career opportunities. Then, out of the blue, she opened a discussion about me with a patron of the café, a man called Hal. Hal always sat playing cards while he ate his food and bantered with the immoral people. But he was different somehow, smartly dressed and quite reserved.

One day he said to me as I ate a sandwich at breakfast, "What are you doing on Saturday?" "Nothing," I replied. "Right," he said. "I'll pick you up at ten in the morning." Sure as day is day, there he was as promised. Not only did he pick me up, he arrived in a beautiful Jaguar. As I sat in the car mesmerized, he quizzed me about my life, my dreams, and my aspirations. Then we went to the cinema. We went for a walk afterward.

I never asked Hal questions myself because I'd learned from my mother years before that Hal owned a prestigious garage that restored VW Beetles. When he dropped me home, he said, "Listen boy, I know things have been tough for you, but you must acquire a skill of some sort or you'll end up like the others I sit with at breakfast in the café." Little did I know that they were all hustlers and thieves—you name it, they were it!

Hal had grown up with them. Although he had chosen a different path, he still had childhood ties and I think his strategy in having breakfast with them was to keep his friends close but his enemies closer. They were so jealous of him. When he'd leave the table I'd have to walk away because of the unkindness of his so-called friends.

After some negotiation with my mother, school officials agreed that, as I was a lad just turning fifteen years old, I could leave school. Dear Hal had me lined up as a panel-beating apprentice at his garage. It would be a two-year apprenticeship, and I would receive a diploma. I would learn a real skill—a skill, he told me, I could use anywhere in the world.

My dear mother had stayed put and networked to get me a chance, and she had accomplished her task. The rest was up to me. Just before I began my apprentice, finally my dear mother had had enough. She presented herself to the council for accommodation. She was given a home about ten miles from the café and arranged the bedrooms so her children could move in. This final departure absolutely broke my father. He became weak, tired, and lifeless. He was so broken, in fact, that I decided to stay put and not move in with Mother.

My younger brother left with Mum, but my sister, who was older than I, also stayed with Father and me. She became hostile and angry with Mother for leaving Father and is still of that opinion today, although she enjoys a pleasant relationship with her.

I completed my two-year apprenticeship at the garage and immediately left to go it alone because I knew I wasn't destined to be an employee forever, and the sooner I got cracking creating my life the better.

Why Me

I rented a lock-up garage as my first place of business. With the few tools I had there, I worked every hour to fix other peoples' vehicles. My goal was to acquire enough money to buy cars from insurance companies that I could repair and sell myself. Within a year, I had built up quite a selection of vehicles for sale, and felt I was heading for success.

Chapter 12

First Born

Whilst all this was happening, my personal life was on hold, although I had met a girl who lived locally. One day she looked me in the face and said, "I'm pregnant." Well, I felt as if I'd been hit by a bolt of lightning. Promptly, I raced to my grandmother to inform her of my conduct and seek guidance—and approval I suppose. She was firm and said, "You put this girl in this position, you've now signed a contract for life to care for another human." She then said, however, "I know you won't let that girl down." "No, Nan," I replied.

It was a wobbly time for me, a seventeen-year-old boy who knew he now had the world ahead on his shoulders. I'd learned another lesson in life: what you create for yourself by your actions creates the life you live for the rest of your life. I remember standing outside the hospital in September 1983 at six o'clock in the morning. My daughter had been born. Although the world had stopped, I stood there thinking, and I knew my

The Medium

life would never be my own again. I was extremely happy but also nervous knowing that responsibility was now the master ruler of my life.

Homeless, and with a young girl and baby, I pleaded with the council to give us a home. Although we lived in a squat for the first year of her life, my daughter gave me immense joy and a reason for everything. It was a bizarre situation, but it turbo charged my ambition and desire.

The journey of fatherhood had begun, and secretly I was terrified. There were no manuals for raising children, and I now had the future of my child in my hands as well as her mother's future and my own. Times were hard—extremely hard—that first year. Profoundly, though my daughter's mother hadn't had the best start in life, she automatically became a great mum, so I knew that, with the love alone from both parents, my daughter would have a good chance. We were always going to do our best.

As I worked through the challenges of fatherhood, I also worked every day in the garage. I would then eat my dinner and go and work as a security guard at a cinema in the evening. At first I worked in West London where there were many unruly teenagers. Then I progressed on to various other venues, and I ended up doing close protection for celebrities and wealthy, paranoid people. It was ironic really. Here was a weedy, battered boy protecting others. It was during this time that I really started connecting with spirits and started relaying messages to people. I was doing cold readings for sitters. My life was consumed with so much, but oddly I just seemed to handle it.

What I didn't realize was that, as I seemed to be growing spiritually, those around me weren't, and this included the mother of my daughter. Sadly, I couldn't give her the attention and love at the level she needed because I'd moved on in so many ways. By the time I had the courage to finally break away, my second daughter had been born. So I had to commit myself to securing their future even though I now felt alone and lonely with no companion to rise with me.

Why Me

I stood by my own word, and both those beautiful daughters became outstanding adults. Obviously, having such a doting mother contributed to their greatness, but I believe I did my share by creating stability and security and by giving my time and my love as best I could while I built a better future. Often I was told I hadn't done enough or been there enough. I often questioned where, how, and when I could have divided myself for the best.

I think, looking back, that although to many I was probably perceived as selfish and too success driven, I knew in my heart of hearts I had to get as far forward as I could before what happened happened, and if I hadn't been that way, all that was possible and all that I achieved for those in my life and myself would not have been possible.

Chapter 13

The Next Stage

From 1983 to 1995, things happened astonishingly fast. I had been in a relationship with a young lady called Maria and believed I was in love until her drinking became nonstop, day and night. This affected my own peace, serenity, and well-being. Maria even told me that I was the reason for her drunkenness, and I almost believed her until I went to the library and read thirty books on alcoholism and realized quickly that I couldn't save the world, or her. I'd become the caretaker, the lost child, and the scapegoat all together. The day I drove her home finally to her mother's house was the day I set myself free, but I also realized I had given up on her, and I must have been the reason she punished herself with drink because she must have felt completely alone due to my selfish business career–oriented lifestyle that years later almost killed me and guided me to where I am today.

I cannot hold myself totally responsible for her pain, as I caused it unknowingly. It was as though I had built my entire life in a trance state. This is probably called narcissism by many, but how could I stop? I was uninformed and knew no different at the time. My spirit team had it planned as had I in my previous lives—the pain, the struggle, and the calamities. How else could a boy of mixed origin, from a broken family, with an odd name, who left school with no exams end up with a multi-million-pound empire consisting of various businesses and properties, and become a pilot capable of flying various types of aircraft? This man put his first daughter through private education and university where she acquired a law degree. Her first home had one bed. Her parents were squatters and had acquired their first mattress from a builder's skip. How could all this be possible for a boy who had been told he was too stupid to fly an aircraft and that he would probably end up being a bum?

Personal advances like mine are possible only with a team, a network of people for support. My team consisted of those who had passed on. Why then, I asked, although to others I seemed arrogant and uncaring, did I privately cry myself to sleep and beg for forgiveness for my mistakes with others. But one day, I lay in a hospital bed and traveled a path with a priest. When I returned, I realized I'm not the teacher of life—of me, of others—I'm just a player, part of a journey. It is the Almighty—by whatever name you my call him—who is in charge of everything.

My grandmother told me about a lady called Mrs. Page, a lady, my grandmother believed, who predicted the future for people. I never met her but hearing about her as a child intrigued me because I also was able to predict the future. But life's struggles seemed to always put my spiritual connection on the back burner as a kind of secondary and unimportant skill. Little did I know that it was controlling everything—my ups, my downs, the good, the bad, the happy, the sad. It allowed me to be built up so high and then to be knocked down so low. Now, I was low, confused by so many materials things, so many so-called friends. Why was I still forging forward but still felt so unhappy? Worse, I had lost the love and togetherness of my family because I was so engulfed in myself and my life. Inside I knew something was terribly wrong, but I had to keep up the façade, and that consumed everything else.

After letting the lady who drank go, I made a decision. I would not work with spirits unknowingly and risk breaking hearts of others even if it was for them to learn the lesson and not me. So I resigned myself to the fact that I would be alone; in other words, I would not allow myself to become attached to a partner or let anyone become attached to me.

I tried being alone for a few years, but I was not successful. I put it down to being a fairly young man. By chance, I bumped into yet another person, a lady at a business venue I was attending. Before I knew it, I was involved in a relationship yet again. It was during this time that the most profound things happened in my life, and it's through my elaboration here about this time, I believe, that most people will benefit. Perhaps they will be able to find association with my story and not make the fundamental mistakes I made. It was, for me, the most glorious chapter of my life.

In summary, at thirty years old, I was at the stage of life where I thought I knew everything. I was totally unbreakable, the world was my oyster, and anything was possible. I had acquired financial stability, not only for the present, but for my early retirement, which, earlier on, I had set as fifty-five. I believed that, at that time, I would resurrect my medium potential and progress it to whatever it had planned for me.

New ventures and businesses were evolving at a rapid rate for me. If I was asked today how I accomplished what I did, I would have to say I wouldn't have a clue. I wouldn't be able to release the formula if I wanted to. Doors were opening for me at a pace usually known only in fiction. The question that was most important to me was, How much was enough? Enough money? Enough adventure? Enough material? Clearly I had many unnecessary materials possessions. How much pretending did I have to do to be a person I didn't even know myself? How could anybody else know who or what I was or had become?

The Medium

You see, I believe life can be like being in the middle of the ocean. You just have to keep swimming or you'll sink—or you'll make yourself believe that to be the case. I genuinely know now that I was secure in my belief that I had everything. In reality, I now know I had nothing. I had fulfilled all my dreams and goals and challenges: I was a competent pilot. Now I knew I wasn't stupid. I wasn't a weedy boy any longer. I had a substantial physique, which had afforded me the opportunity to play a part in a television production for a brief period. You see, I was being driven by total insecurity and a need to be important. The strange thing is that I was not important for a single moment. I was alive only for myself, not even my children, and this was sad because I now I had three, and there was one on the way.

I still hadn't learned the essence of life because I hadn't learned about myself. I thought I needed to learn only about everyone else. Life, I believe, is given to us to create. The creating journey is learned only once we have mastered and created by whatever means available to us. I only created, and I created many things, but they were always to my detriment in some way.

I have no regrets. I don't sat this out of arrogance; rather, I say it because I know that everything was meant to be, everything happened for a reason.

Chapter 14

My Hero

Everybody has a hero. Mine was my nan, not because she was wiser, richer, bigger, stronger, fatter, thinner, and more clever, respected, and trusted than others. She wasn't those things to me either. I believe she was my hero because, no matter what I was or was going to be, she loved me without condition, without judgement, without reason, without method or madness.

One evening we sat, squished together, in her armchair drinking Horlicks. She said, with a tear in her eye, "If only I knew not to make all the mistakes I've made when I was your age, I wouldn't have carried such a heavy load. So, as you walk through life growing up, if you care, people will know. They may shout at you and you at them but deep down inside they will forgive you, and you will forgive them. For if they are caring people like you must learn to be, they will be going through learning processes too.

The Medium

All people must learn it at some stage in their lives. But I believe that people learn only when the time is right and they are ready. People must be ready to receive others and must be ready to give to others. It's all about timing.

One day some twenty add years later, I received a call from my mother. She said, "You'd better come here, son. Your Nan is about to go." I will never forget that call; I was sitting on the toilet when it came through.

With haste, I raced through the streets of London, begging the spirits not to take her until I arrived. When I arrived at the house, my two aunties, Carrie and Maria, and my mother greeted me at the door. "Can I see her? Is she okay?" "Yes," my mother replied. "She's weak," Carrie said. "We'll let you know when you can go in to her," Maria said.

Well, my Nan heard my voice as I stood in the hall, and I heard her ask for me. As I opened the door, I looked down at the little grey armchair to my right. It was the same chair in which we used to squish together as we ate butterscotch and talked. It was empty now. I looked across to the bed that was now accommodating her. It had been brought downstairs because she was so ill and needed so much care.

So kindly, her daughters—all three of them—allowed me to have a final good-bye with my Iron Lady. My whole world was that lady, as she had been to so many. As I knelt beside her and held her hand, she smiled and said. "I've been waiting for you. I can't do it anymore. I can't. It hurts so much." As my eyes filled up, I felt such pain deep in my soul. I said, "Let go. Don't punish yourself. Even the doctors have said how you have fought. It is remarkable." With that, tears rolled down both her cheeks, and she said, "I can't go. I can't. What will you do? Nobody understands you truly, only me. What will you do without me?" You see, nobody knew except her that she was right. Nobody did know me. She was the only person I could really talk to, and she understood me so well. Even to this day, I truly believe that hasn't changed.

With a hard-to-adopt, stiff upper lip I said, "Nan, I'll be okay. I promise." But in my heart, I knew I wouldn't, and I wasn't. Bending close to her ear, I whispered softly, "Nan, I love you. Go when you're ready, but please don't worry about me. In any case, the worst that can happen is I'll stay here and not be with you again for a long time." She turned her little frail face to me and said, "You must know this: I promise I will always watch over you." Again a tear rolled from her eye, and as I felt her soft, freckled hands, which had comforted me for my whole life, I knew I'd touch them no more after that day, and that knowledge sent fear through me as if I was a small boy left standing in the center of the world with not a single human left on earth.

I kissed her head again for the final time, walked into the breakfast room, and kissed my grandfather, Henry, who was sitting staring into space. He also knew his soulmate was about to start her journey to the unknown. I told him I loved him and left.

As I drove back through the dark streets of London, I screamed out loud in my car, "Why? Why take her so young?" You see, she had a swift tongue, but everyone loved her. She may not have been popular, but she was always respected.

For the next few days I became subdued. I couldn't speak to anybody. I lost my appetite and felt so lonely that, even when I surround myself with people, they made me feel as though I was empty.

My mother called me and said, "Your Nan is at the undertakers. Would you like to see her one last time?"

Collecting my courage, I sat on the train and traveled to the undertakers'. I sat in a daze as the train stopped at a station and approximately twenty youths got on, shouting and demanding valuables from all the passengers, who were sitting quietly. They moved through the train bullying people, and I looked up as they were looming even more closely to me. Strangely, when they came near to where I was sitting, lost and alone, I felt no fear. I looked straight ahead and as though I was invisible. they just walked straight past me and got off at the next stop. I didn't even

The Medium

really think about it at the time—the danger I was in. How could I have just sat there? Was it a dream?

When I arrived at the undertakers', I was greeted by my dear sweet mother. She said, "You okay, love?" "Yes," I replied as she guided me into my Nan's resting place. I again touched her cold, precious hands and kissed her forehead, saying, "I'll miss you, Nan, like the world will never know."

She was cremated a short while after that, and I feared for Grandad Henry because he looked as though he was a fish out of water. Here was a man who had privately told me stories about his time in the war and who had shared his love for Churchill and all his adventures. It was heartbreaking to see him so sad. For the next few weeks, I found myself being asked by people "What's up?" I had always been a boy and a man who never stopped talking. Now I was quiet, and people seemed more and more worried about me.

One day, with an exceptionally heavy heart, I drove to Alexandra Palace, stopped the car, and sat staring over at the highest point. As I shed a tear, I heard a voice say, "I haven't gone, but you will unless you start eating again." With that, I looked to my left and saw my dear Nan sitting next to me. I spoke to her, explaining all my fears and worries. By the time she told me that everything would be okay, I looked up to see it was dark. Six hours had passed as though in a millisecond. I drove home, and for the first time in months, I believed I would be facing my next life adventure.

Chapter 15

The Next Adventure

Home at that time was a bedsit, which I shared with my lady who was always drunk. I had bought a shop with a three-bedroom flat above it, as my two daughters and their mother needed a place to live. The girls' mum wanted to have a career as the girls were both in school by now. My father guaranteed the loan for that first shop, believe it or not. He helped me to acquire it because, no matter how much money a person had, if a person had no property or credit history, landlords wouldn't consider entering into a contract.

I had been trying to forgive my father. I craved a father-son relationship, and things were improving because I'd now made him a grandfather. I was slowly learning his language through friends I'd made who were from his country of birth.

Everything was going so well until he remarried and had another child with his new wife. Slowly he began to change. He became hostile and aggressive once again. The only difference now was that I was six foot three and could defend myself. So, once again, I gave up that dream of happy father and son.

I enrolled in various business courses to help the mother of my two daughters expand the High Street shop, and soon I owned a shared house with her. I believed that would stop her drinking; however, it got worse than ever, so I moved out again into a bedsit hoping to find some serenity.

By chance one day, I met a grey-haired lady in a shop who stopped me and said, just out of the blue, "Use your gift. It's time." And then she walked off. I ran after her and asked her what she meant. She replied, "Use your intuition, and all your dreams will come true."

That was hard for me because I'd always been told by my father I was a big ape and would achieve nothing. All I would ever produce were just big ideas.

Maybe, maybe! I thought. *Ideas can materialize!* So I started visualizing all I wanted for myself and those I loved. I was a bit cautious because my big ideas had caused me to become estranged from my two lovely aunties. My mouth was too sharp, you see, when I was a child, and they were brought up to believe children should be seen but not heard. I thought, *What have I got to lose?* I began to work hard each day. I dreamed and planned and designed. I went back to night school to improve my math skills, to pass my pilot exams, then to further my studies in business management and design.

This time I kept my mouth shut. But little did I know that not telling others what you're up to only creates rumors and gossip. People misinterpreted my behavior and perceived sinister goings on, especially as nobody understood my gift. My gift was all I was going on. I was being guided and counselled by the deceased, my Nan being the main guide.

People flocked to me like seagulls to a fisherman. Within ten years I had amassed a great network of business partners. Unfortunately, I stupidly mistook many of these people as friends—except for a handful. As the saying goes, if you can count your friends on one hand, you're lucky. I judged people by my own standards and thought they would be eternally grateful for all they achieved with me as I did with them.

However, my heart was heavy because I had still not found my one true love. The drinker had gone, and I had now committed personally and in business to another lady. Although my mother had said to me some years earlier, "Son, if you're going to fall in love, you'll meet your girl in a shop doorway."

As my empire grew I became obsessed with wanting more, more, more! How much was enough? If I'd had a brain, I'd have stopped. I was amassing wealth but causing my soul and my spirit to decay. I was simply a working machine for business and acquisition. Some would have called me a horrible person, self-centered and uncaring.

Upon waking up one day, I realized that I had everything materially around me and could make any choice at the drop of a hat, but who was I? And, more importantly, who was I to others?

We are taught not to care what others think. *But why is that?* I asked myself. Surely, a person is nothing to this world if he or she is not liked and loved by others. So, rather than change radically, I started watching not only myself, but others. I thought I had many friends around me who really loved me for me, understood part of my being, and allowed me into their lives for me, not for them. Then I started to realize that perhaps I had fooled them, for deep down in my heart, I knew I wasn't revealing the real me.

I bought a house that backed onto a valley. It was an old house, and the previous owners had lived there for seventy-five years.

One day I walked into the small local airport and asked if I could meet the resident helicopter pilot. The man picked up the phone and called somebody. Ten minutes later, a handsome James Bond–type chap walked through the door, and with a smile on his face said, "Hello, hello!" I'll never forget him. He'd just finished his lunch—a tuna sandwich—and boy could I smell the tuna! Some years later we had a chat about the fact that you never get a second chance to make a first impression. But that fishy smell hadn't dampened this chap's presence!

The Medium

This was a new opportunity for me—a new friend, a person to whom I could show the real me. Well, after our first flight together that day, somehow I knew I was going to learn to love this man, and I did. We would spend hours together, sometimes like two teenage girls, sharing our most intimate fears. As he grew over the years, so did our friendship and trust in each other.

It was bizarre. He arrived in my life at this time because I was in total emotional turmoil because I realized I had brought a lady into my life when I was at a low point, and I had soon realized I wasn't for her. Worse, I loved her father very much and had given him my word that I would take care of her, and I was a man of my word. Even worse, she was an honest girl from a good family, and I felt I had led her along.

Every time I thought I was ready to make the wrong right, somehow I couldn't, so things got worse. I was living a lie. I'd given my word. How could I say to this lady I'd made a mistake and wasted her time and love on me? How could I go back on my word to her father and mother? I tried to pretend I was happy, and I beat myself up daily. How could I not be happy with a good, honest family girl like that? I felt so ungrateful and confused. To fall in love with someone, you focus on all the things you like about the person. To fall out of love, you focus on all the things you don't like. What made it worse for me was that this lady liked—or said she liked—everything I liked. This made it terribly difficult for me to fault her in the beginning even though I knew in my heart that I was wasting her time.

I used to fly into a lovely place with my dear friend, Jason, he was also a pilot, and we'd eat Stilton burgers there and chat about life's challenges and adventures past and present. All he wanted was to be a dad, but he couldn't quite settle with the right lady. One day when we were at this place, I'd got up to answer my phone. As I walked out the door, I blinked and suddenly, a lady appeared in front of me in a doorway. She seemed assertive, but she had a shrunken aura. My mother had been right. Within a millisecond, I knew above and beyond anything else that, within this doorway, stood my life partner. It was a though the part of me that had been missing had suddenly joined me, making me complete. As she stood facing me, awaiting me to step back to let her pass, I said without hesitation or thinking, "Wow! You're a pretty thing!" When I think about that, I realize it was corny and rubbish to refer to the mightiest lady who would ever enter my life a "thing"!

She smiled and walked past. I mumbled into the phone. My friend, Jason, had heard what I'd said. As he walked up behind me, he said, "What did you say?" I replied, "I've got to go, Jason. I've just seen my love of my life—the woman I'm going to marry." "Oh dear," he replied. "Don't let another woman get to your heart."

I ended the call and walked back into the restaurant only to see her standing at the bar. I walked over and stood beside her. As I tried to make her acquaintance, her leg buckled. I kind of caught her and asked if she was all right. Little did I know, I was about to go on the biggest journey of love, loss, sadness, and self-discovery with this lady.

I was leaving the next day for a business trip. I gave her my number which was unlike me because I rarely gave my number to a complete stranger, but from that minute on I could not get her out of my mind. That, too, was unlike me. Even the macho, arrogant side of me didn't stop me from contacting her immediately on my arrival abroad. Worse, I almost felt as if I'd left half of me behind. I felt I had to return as soon as possible. By the time I returned home, I had already arranged a meeting. My head was cloudy, and I was telling myself I might be stupid. Once I'd had dinner with her and looked her in the eye, I might want to walk away and continue the life I'd committed to. However, as we sat and ate, I was consumed with her. I even started saying nonsense like, "I don't want commitment." But, as I said it, I thought, *What on earth are you saying?*

As I drove her home, I thought, *I don't want to let her out of my sight.* I almost felt that parting from her would leave her vulnerable to the horrid world I knew. That night I drove back to the other side of London, checked into a hotel where I often stayed, and started thinking. As I sat in the chair next to the bed, I looked up. There, again, sat my dear Nan. I asked her, "What on earth should I do now?"

She smiled and said, "I've been waiting for this to happen. Now I can go off to explore because I know you won't be lonely. This lady has been waiting to join you, and you have been waiting to join her, yet neither of you even knew it. You must be patient with her; she has a few things to sort out before she realizes you need only each other." Then she said, "Whatever you do, don't let her go. If you do, you'll both be lost—maybe forever."

So, happy as a child dancing over the cracks in the pavement, each day I'd yearn to be in her presence again. Each time I was, I felt alive and complete. Finally I grew the courage to go back on my word and set the other lady in my life free. She had never given me reciprocal love.

My mate was often away working; she was a trained stage artist. I always said to her before she left, as I held her tight, "Stay loyal. Don't doubt me or my love. All our dreams will come true." Her problem was that she was extremely loyal, and she had abusive parents. They used guilt tactics to force her to work when and where and for how long they planned. They probably hoped that, one day, she'd hit the big time and settle them for life. Because they had put the time in with her, she felt obliged to pay and pay and comply with all their demands.

Then problems arose. She didn't even know it, and neither did I at the time. Because I had her heart, I was her parents' enemy. I could corrupt their plans and, worse, expose the awful, wicked way they had exploited her as they raised her. I could take it no more. I knew I had to step up and step away. I wanted to be free to fly away with my love. But then I was told that she was pregnant, and I had to comfort her as she was having the baby. All I can remember were my Nan's words in 1983 about children, "Son, you've got an obligation and a job for life."

She gave birth to a beautiful boy; however, he was extremely ill with a serious genetic blood disorder when he was born. What a position to be in! How could I say, "I don't love you. I love somebody else"? How could I leave her alone with an ill child? The next year was torture. Although I let her pretend to the world that we were together, I was always somewhere else, usually with my love or at work. I joined her only to accommodate her needs for my son and to continue the façade we had created for people close by.

The following year, my true love gave birth to a beautiful daughter. I had committed to finding her a home long before because her parents had beaten her badly and thrown her out on the street. I spent as much time there with her in between working expeditions. That was the happiest part of my life. But, inside, I was dying. I knew I was living a lie to the one I loved—I hadn't told her about my son. Each day I'd wake feeling terrible, living a lie. I also lived with the daily fear of having a little boy who was so ill. Each day I'd pray to God, asking him to make my son well so he could grow strong. I also asked that I be freed from the web that tangled around me further each day.

All my life I'd felt free. My soul had always been calm no matter what life threw at me. But now I felt trapped, afraid, insecure, unkind, sad, and lost. But the world perceived me as a high-flying Tycoon who used people to accommodate my flash, self-centered, have-all, have-everyone lifestyle.

As the years rolled on, I immersed myself deeper and deeper into multiple business acquisitions. In reality, I was smothering the pain and sadness. I was hiding the creation of a quadruple life, and doing it in such a way that I didn't have to lie. I was splitting myself and dividing and pretending. My huge fear of people being hurt because of my doing and creating and knowing someday would have to come out. I wished so much that I wouldn't care, but I did, and those sad feelings wouldn't go away. One day my love felt she had to understand what was going on, and she pushed for answers. It seemed as though whichever way I turned, people were going to get hurt, and nothing could stop it. Months turned into years. So much happened, but what never changed was my love for my lady.

The Medium

I knew my lady was in a place of no return, so one day, while sitting alone eating a lonely burger at lunch in a small café in London, I closed my eyes and said, "Whoever you are, wherever you may be, enough! Do with me what you will. I cannot go on any further with this façade." By this time, I realized that, the more I planned to make things right, the worse they became. *But, I asked myself, why have I achieved such success with business and financial security if I am a terrible person when it comes to looking after other peoples' hearts?*

I turned to my dear friend, Jason. As we were flying one day, I asked him, "Do you think our journeys are mapped out?" "Yes," he said. He had always shared his story with me. One day he had stood looking at a beautiful, large helicopter at a particular prestigious landing site. This was long before he could fly. On that day, he said to himself, *One day, I will fly from here in one of those helicopters. That is my purpose, my dream, my goal. Anything after that will be a bonus because, when I can fly, I will have achieved my ultimate personal goal.*

His advice to me was, "Nothing really matters." He said this as he patted his head and said, "Look, we break. We are nothing really, and nothing is real." Then he did his signature bit of naughty saying, "Look, shall we head down there and pick wild mushrooms?" We had done that many times. It was naughty because it took us off our planned schedule.

What I didn't realize at the time was that I had been ignoring my spiritual gift. More and more, day by day, I had not been listening or even caring enough to see the signs. I was just lost in a world of denial and pushing on.

Chapter 16

Absent Friends

At this time, I must mention those I haven't mentioned, not because they weren't important. They were important, and I respect and thank all those souls for all they contributed to my life, good or bad. I do sometimes wonder, though, where they were when I was finally ripped to the bone when I lost absolutely everything including, almost, my life. But in my heart, I say friends and family members are sometimes meant to be with us for our lifetimes and sometimes for just a short duration.

It was a cold winter's day in the winter of 2003 as I sat at my desk in the morning. I called Jason, and we talked. He said he'd spent enough time flying, and now he wanted something different. "What?" I asked. "What would you like to do?" He said he didn't know because all his dreams had been fulfilled. It was as though he had lost his zest, his life, his ambitions, his drive, and his passion. Although I never showed it, I also felt the same.

The Medium

A few months passed and, as usual, I was as busy as ever. One day I received a phone call. Jason had been in an accident. As my heart raced, repeated the usual visualizations: "Be positive. All will be okay. He'll be fine." I repeated this to myself anxiously. Later, I felt numb as it was confirmed that he was gone. I cried as we buried him. After he was laid to rest, I drove home.

Soon, the shock took hold of me. I had been somewhat prepared for the passing of my grandparents and for others I'd lost through illness. I'd had time to accept their passing. But when I lost someone I dearly loved, and it happened as quick as a phone call, I became literally stopped in time.

Jason had been true to his word. He'd flown that day from that base in that aircraft he'd said he would. After losing him, I didn't eat. I couldn't speak. People were shouting at me, pleading for me to take charge of business issues. Things could easily go wrong; my associates needed me to function.

What I wasn't telling anyone was that I had been talking to the deceased, learning from them. With them I experienced no lies, no deceit, no cheating, no fabrication, no unkind jealousy, no cruel words. We just spoke of love and the why of things—why it is so important to accept that nothing is real, time is short, and time waits for no man or woman.

Life is supposed to teach us lessons—nothing more, nothing less. The lessons are about ourselves. Other people teach us lessons, and we teach other people lessons. Sometimes we teach with kindness and sometimes with pain. Life is a process. Our environment and everything in it contribute as we play out the learning games of life.

I returned some months later to reality, resigned to the fact that I wasn't in control of my destiny; it was in control of me based on what situation I was or wasn't putting myself in. I just ploughed on as usual believing that everything would fall into place soon in some way or form if I just aligned myself with people and places that my intuition guided me to.

You see, again, I had no choice; I was in the same position in life—way over my head. I just had to believe, wish no harm to another, and pray that my good intentions would be fruitful even if I had to suffer further pain. I had not lost my dearest friend, my true love and soulmate, my dear grandmother. Who or what else, I thought, could I possibly lose? So I swam in the ocean of my life, although now I was truly lost and alone. I thought I'd just keep on swimming for the sake of it. What would be would be.

The only thing that I knew was that the mess was of my own creation. Also, everything was financially secure because of my creation—or so I thought.

By 2007, I started to feel unwell. At first I had migraine headaches every day for months on end. In between attacks, I worked to catch up as best I could. Little did I know that something was going terribly wrong in my stomach. One Monday morning, I left my hotel room after being shut away for three days of migraines. I headed for the office thinking, *I've had enough! When is Fate going to free me from all this pressure?* I worked that week and decided I would take on no more projects in any area; in fact, I thought of starting to sell up, reducing and simplifying all aspects of my life.

On the following Saturday, I drove to see a dear friend and medium I had known since I was a young man. On my arrival, as though he knew I was coming he said, "I've been waiting for you." As I sat with him, he said, "It's time for you to change. Everything is positioned for you to change. Everything is planned for you. Listen, there are spirits around you. Let them guide you."

I left and walked to a shop where I bought a book on positivity. I quickly realized that, as long as I believed that I and all those I loved would be okay, then we would be okay. When I say okay, I mean we would have the ability to see through all imbalance and mess.

I fought on for another few months. I was extremely tired and losing weight. Finally I admitted myself to hospital because the pain in my intestines was unbearable. The first day I lay in the bed, I felt free at last. I was approaching the end, or so I though at the time. I was almost pleased I'd become so unwell. It was my chance to be free from the extreme pressures that were hounding me on a daily basis from every angle. Ultimately, it was my chance to rest from being hands on 24/7, running multiple businesses and living a hectic lifestyle. For the first time in twenty odd years I felt as if the weight of the world was lifting from my shoulders. Any illness I had to fight surely couldn't be worse than that.

However, I was down to seven stone (ninety-eight pounds) and gravely ill. The medicines that were prescribed over the coming months to save my life eroded my heart and bones. Nothing for nothing as the saying goes. What was happening? I felt different. I was losing my ego, and ego creatives drive, success, desire, and acquisition. However, my ego was also driving away insecurities and providing me with a sense of self-worth, which was visible to others. As I was being stripped back to the bone, I felt calm and a real sense of freedom, so much so that the calm that was growing enabled me to even accept I that I might pass. That would be okay.

Several doctors stood over me one day. One of them said, "We need to give you a blood transfusion. If we don't start administering it in the next few hours, you will be in grave danger." I really didn't realize how ill I was because I felt such calm and peace within me. "No," I replied. "No transfusion. What will be will be." You see, a blood transfusion meant that I might get well. Then I would have to go back to my old life, and that terrified me more than passing over. Then I thought, *What about my love and my children?*

Well, the children grow up and leave you someday, and I'd lost my love, the girl I'd waited for all my life. She tried constantly telling me she hadn't left, but she had, having been influenced by her atrocious family members and so-called friends. What she didn't realize was that, when she left, even though it was for a few weeks, in those few weeks she severed my soul, and my soul had been connected to all my dreams, which saw the two of us as one.

I later realized that was nonsense; again, it was just my ego taking over. As I thought I'd formulated my final thoughts, the

Why Me

doctor stepped out of the room and a priest appeared. Well, I thought, *It really must be my time if they are sending priest in.* He stood calmly beside the bed and said, "May I talk with you?" "Why?" I asked. "Because you owe it to yourself to have a chat with me." His soft voice calmed me as I took in his white hair and pleasant smile. There was a picture on the wall at the end of the bed. I had stared at it so often during my hospitalization. As I glanced over at it then, I saw my grandmother looking at me. She said, "Are you sure you're ready? You can do anything you put your mind to." This was just what she'd always said to me throughout my life. It was funny, but I also felt as though the room was full of people. I could feel the hustle and bustle, but I couldn't see them.

With that the priest said, "Why don't you get up? Maybe you could sit in the chair for a bit or even take a slow walk." As he held out his hand, I got up and stood beside him. *Strange*, I thought. I'd been unable to get out of that bed for weeks. He held my hand and said, "Come along. Just walk slowly." As I walked out the door, the corridor seemed longer than I knew it to be and much brighter. It was almost as though spot lights were being shone from the other end toward us. He smiled and slowly guided me saying, "All will be fine. Now see? You're walking again. Just take a few more steps." I felt so well, so lovely, so warm. As we approached the end of the corridor, I couldn't see anything. All of a sudden, as if in a split second, I watched my whole life's happiest times flash before me.

Two things immediately stayed in my thoughts. First, I saw myself sitting in front of my love. She was crying, holding a teddy bear I had bought for her. Second, all my children—all of them—were sitting in a circle around a picture of me. They were just staring not saying a word. I said to the priest, "Wait. I'm not ready. Please go and tell the doctor I'll have the transfusion." "Okay," he said. I looked down at the floor and closed my eyes, thinking how selfish I was being willing to leave those I loved when I still had fight in me. As I opened my eyes, I was crying, and I was back in bed. Doctors and nurses were running around talking loud and fast. The room was full of hustle and bustle. How had I got back in bed so quickly? I felt that I'd been with that priest for ages, and we had been way down the corridor.

I looked at the nurse and said, "Where has the priest gone? I want to thank him and say good-bye." "What priest?" she said. "We can't insert the IV because your veins are too fragile. We're going to have to try in uncomfortable places. Is that okay?"

They found some good veins, and as the days passed, the new blood kept on coming. As I recovered, I felt I was like a baby again. Even using my mouth to swallow soup fed to me was new. It took months to relearn all bodily movement, especially learning to walk again. But somehow I persevered through the good and bad days, the ups and the downs, just as I'd done my whole life.

I stupidly refused visitors, even my love. This was probably because I never wanted to be seen and remembered that way just in case I didn't pull through.

Chapter 17

Everything Is Taken

The day came for me to leave the hospital. I wasn't truly ready or strong enough, but the doctors had said if I didn't go then, I never would. Cabin fever was setting in. Fear engulfed me like a massive tidal wave. *I can't,* I thought. *I can't face everyone and the problems I know spiritually are going to be there. What has become of my life's work, my security, my world?* I had always been at the helm, directing everything, keeping it all together. The doctors agreed I could leave in stages, taste the world outside again, and return as and when I needed to. Well, I did that for almost five years, probably because the doctors also knew that, after my initial recovery, my insides would take at least five years to recover.

As I started to rebuild my body, stabilize, and heal, I watched as piece by piece of my life's work—my security, my safety—crumbled and fell. The banks and the creditors and all the people involved dissected my world until, finally, I was left with a suitcase of personal belongings and my clothes.

The first loss was the hardest. Bizarrely, after that, after each loss, I felt a strange calm. I was almost happy to surrender, to pass over my property. I felt no arrogance. I had no fight, no desire. As each piece was taken, a part of me grew. I had worked hard to erect each of those buildings. I though my children's children's children would one day say, "My great-grandad build those buildings. He started with nothing, only a little shop his father secured for him to give his children a safe area to live in." Losing was hard because, to everyone else, my dreams were nothing—easy come, easy go. The bricks and mortar to me, however, had been my dreams, my creations, my whole life's work, and they were being dismantled and destroyed.

What the doctors didn't tell me was that, when they finally kicked me out of hospital after years of medication and pain killers, and after years of existing in the noisy hospital hustle and bustle, my sleep patterns would be inconsistent and my body would not easily adjust to a sudden cessation of medicines. The shock of that alone could have killed me. So I had to deal with these new health issues along with the huge loses of material things. I also lost friends and people I had thought were friends, and even family members. I thought these people would never leave me, but they all disappeared one by one, each resituating himself or herself, setting up new adventures because I had no more adventures to offer them. I even totally accepted that my time in their lives had passed along with my time with them.

I felt like a lone seagull with a broken wing, vulnerable and afraid, sitting on an iceberg in Antarctica. I remembered something I once had read: "Only for today." That truly kept me alive. The one thing I focused on was the thing that worked, and that was my mind. As long as that worked, I'd be okay. Although I had lost so much and felt so sad, I realized I still had small children and my love who never gave up on me through my weakest times.

Why Me

Even as a small boy, I loved children. I always adored their innocence and truthfulness. It is only life that corrupts their minds, not themselves. So here I was, a broken man with nothing. I felt no regrets. I had no scores to settle. Although I did initially begin a huge law suit against the bank, I soon realized my energy was being lost in the fight. So I decided to focus on the future.

Chapter 18

The Future

I decided to focus on what I had and not what I didn't have. I had a lady and children. I believed they loved me; they had never given up on me. My gift, also, had never left me. I still had the ability to talk to and listen to the dead, I started to feel safe again. The deceased now had a stronger connection with me because, just like them, I held no anger, no greed, no desire to acquire anything but love and kindness. As I started to learn about myself, I learned that life is a process of learning. It is nothing more, nothing less. Without my lessons, all those buildings would have meant nothing to my children, but if I could teach my children the deeper understanding of life, rather than what the rat race of society expects of us, perhaps when the time again occurs for me to pass, my journey would not have been in vain.

I made a pact with myself that, day after day from then on, I would make a conscious effort to not be distracted by any external pull back into the rat race, which is governed by peer pressure, acquisition, and greed. The first step was to acquire a disciplined plan, a regime of finding daily time to meditate. Mediation is the way to finding one's higher, inner self. It allows you to step out of your daily thoughts and into a cleaner, clearer, open-hearted place. It is the basis of a clear, clean platform where we can find peace and tranquility. We can develop creatively that can enable us to experience a fresh outlook at all that's going on and has gone on and what you'd like to go on in your life. Just sitting quietly, breathing, focusing on your breath can have a tremendous effect on your physical and mental well-being. It helps clear and recharge your mind.

What I also found, for myself, was that meditation quickly helped me connect and choose which spirits I could talk with. I was even able to request specific individuals from whom I could seek guidance and advice.

So here I was, a man who had been battered and traumatized by life's goings on. But I had survived. I knew I wanted a peaceful present and future life. But how could I live in a sort of monk-like state with all life's hustle and bustle and challenges around me and still provide the basic, fundamental, and essential needs for myself and my family—housing, clothes, and food. With no clear plan of how I was going to survive, I was determined not to be sucked back into the old ways and old lifestyle. I had lost everything, as I said, except the house I now lived in, which I had acquired at the height of my success—or the origin of my demise, I should say.

Luckily, there were a few very special people who helped me keep my life going long enough for me to find my new path and direction. It was hard because so many would say something like, "Come on! Get going again! You're a creator, a business man. Get started with business again!" They badgered me not knowing, bless them, that my new path was deeper than that. How could I explain that I had different plans? How could I explain that I was waiting for the new journey to be formed? They would have thought I'd gone barmy.

The house I was dwelling in began to be the source of my growth. The more I lost, the more I grew. I sat tight in this knowledge. I began to search the history of this home and found out it had always created challenges for all its previous occupants. Some had found great material success while living there; some had overcome great personal challenges. I started to realize I wasn't there by accident. I was there to learn about the real me and what my real purpose in life was.

I did, however, know that the time would come for me to leave. One night, I woke to hear my daughter crying and shouting, "No, No! I don't want to play! I want to sleep." I went into the room where she slept with her sister, who was sound asleep. I saw a small spirit girl—the same girl who had lived in a house I had lived in twenty years earlier. I had been told by the previous occupants of that house that the house was haunted by a child. What I didn't realize was that, because I had been able to talk to her in spirit, she had decided to follow me to my new home. However, I had not seen her since leaving my previous home twenty years before. As I walked into the room that night, I said, "What are you doing here? Why are you disturbing my daughter?" "I want to play," she said. "I've waited for you to have more children so I could play. Other children can't see or hear me." After we talked for a while, we agreed that she wouldn't bother my daughter unless my daughter was happy to have a reciprocal dialogue.

As I turned to walk down the stairs, the spirit girl said, "What about Ralph? Aren't you going to speak with him?" As she spoke, a man appeared in front of me in the hall. He seemed to be in his early sixties. He was about five five, was very thin, and was wearing a dark suit. I tried to talk with him, but he just scowled at me. He said nothing, and as I walked past him, he just shook his head.

As time went by, no matter what I did, I just couldn't save a penny living in that house. One day, out of the blue, my lady told me there a was a spiritual fair going on in an area where I used to live. She was interested in the paranormal, and I had been reading for her randomly for years. She said she would like to go to the fair because there was a psychic artist who would be demonstrating a camera that could capture an image of a person's aura.

Chapter 19

The Psychic Fair

I hadn't been to a fair of this sort previously, and I thought it might be a pleasant and interesting experience. My worry was that admission was expensive; however, on our arrival, as we stood in the queue at the doors, bizarrely we were handed some free entry tickets for our entire family. We walked among stalls displaying paraphernalia, and we saw some demonstrations. Finally, we arrived at the aura camera display. I must say I had no intention to be involved in any kind of demonstration, but the photographer presented himself to me and asked if I would I like a sitting. "No," I replied, "but my wife would." He advised us to return in approximately twenty minutes. "By the way," he said, "I think you should have a sitting, too, when you return."

When we returned for my lady's sitting, she seemed excited. When it was over, she was able to hold a picture of her aura. The photographer interpreted the image and told her about her tendencies and character, together with her spiritual awareness,

The Medium

reception, and ability. She encouraged me to have a sitting also, so I sat before the photographer. He looked at me directly in the face and said, "Before we begin, do you know why you're here doing this?" "Yes," I replied as though I had been waiting for this moment all my life. I felt, for the first time in my life, appreciated, loved, and known. This feeling was unlike anything I had ever felt before. The camera produced an image of my aura that was a full, deep purple. The photographer said he could see evidence of my spirituality among other personal traits and associated patterns. I took the photographer's card and bid him thank you and farewell. Nothing more was said. When we returned home, I felt compelled immediately to contact this photographer again.

As usual, I didn't make haste. I waited for several weeks, thinking it through; however, the impulse to contact him became stronger by the day. When I finally called him, he invited me to meet him to discuss possibilities and opportunities for further understanding and possible development. He told me initially that I already knew about myself. He told me that he was a medium himself, and he could teach me. He said I should attend classes to perfect my ability to deliver professional mediumship. I agreed, and for the next six months, I attended lessons every week, he called it finishing school of which he delivered to me personally. The lessons were incredible. They covered so many topics related to mediumship, even legalities like the 1951 Fraudulent Medium Act. I learned about the history of mediumship and empathic loving, and I learned how to work with spirits. I learned to ask for evidence and not just receive it at random when the spirits decided to dump it on me.

Well, I had always been a strange child. Ironically, my family members, and later my wife, even described me as obsessed. If I became interested in a subject, I'd study it to exhaustion. Even when I was eight or nine years old, I'd travel on buses and trains across London to research my newfound interest or obsession. I once wanted to learn about fish. I learned all the Latin names and the behavior of each specie until I convinced myself I was expert enough in that field to hold discussions for hours. As the years went by, I obsessed about and learned about many subjects, always trying to master the topic. There were no computers in those days, only libraries. And I loved talking to experts in my chosen fields.

The downfall for me was that my excitement about the subject matter would irritate my parents and family members. They would say, "You talk too much! It's always about you!" I know now that, if they had really listened or given me chance to explain, they would understand that it wasn't about me; it was what I wanted and was learning about.

The subjects changed so fast because I consumed information at a speedy pace and moved on to new topics and back to previous ones. I was called a five-minute wonder child because I didn't seem to finish with any given interest. Perhaps other children just pursue one chosen subject of interest. I would stop being interested in one subject and proceeded to another. I might put the first subject on hold because library resources and experts were limited to me. I always returned my original subjects when more study opportunities became available again.

I now understand that my brain was constantly searching for new information, and the only person who understood this about me was my grandmother. She used to say to me quietly, "Your brain learns faster than most people's. They can't keep up, so they switch off." What I didn't realize was that her comments and encouragement, which I was so thrilled to receive, were what increased my ego. Yes, ego—the thing that destroys men and women alike. Years later I had to dance with death before it would be curtailed. I say curtailed because I believe you can never truly eliminate it from your being. I know this because I watched my own sister and her ego from the time she was a very early age. Her ego took over so much in later years that she became hostile toward me. She even committed the cardinal family sin of slandering me to others, even strangers.

I understand, but she didn't understand me or even herself, bless her. Her fabricated tales about me painted a picture of untruth to others, and this hurt me. I still send her love and good

The Medium

thoughts as I search for knowledge and learning. What I didn't realize was how I had put myself in danger by not recognizing that all humans don't have good intentions. As I was growing and learning, I was broadening my geographical stomping ground, which meant meeting and mingling with all kinds of people. Some were good some were bad. How was I to know who was who and what was what until I actually spent some time with these people and groups? I'd find myself sometimes around certain folks, and after a while, I'd think, *Goodness their intentions are not the kind I want to be associated with*. When I found myself in that position, I would have to find a way to detach myself and remove myself from their company.

For example, I once met a group of friends near a club I used to go to of an evening. They were Air Cadets. They never went to that club, but they always used to hang around outside. As I left the club one day, they asked if I'd like to join them at their local snooker club the next evening. I liked pool, so I agreed. "Meet us here tomorrow at five in the evening," one of them said. On my arrival the next day, two of these boys were there. They seemed rather strange, almost in a drunken like state. One produced two packets of crisps and gave me one. "Thank you," I kindly replied. He then responded, "Eat the crisps. The best bit is afterward." I indulged, and when we had finished our crisps, he produced a large tube of glue and started filling the bag. As I stood watching, I thought, *Gosh what is he going to do with that?* It wasn't until he started breathing into the bag a few times as his face turned red that I thought, *Oh, no! What am I involved in now?* He removed the bag from his face and offered to fill mine up. "No thank you," I replied. "You must," he said. "It's the only way to talk to the dancing miniature people—the ones you can't usually see. It's the only way to see ghostly faces." "No," I again replied, and he turned more aggressive as he insisted. Finally I assured him, "I can see other people without that." Well that was it. By this time, the other boy was intoxicated and hallucinating and furious at my comment. I could see what they saw; and I didn't have to do such awful sniffing. As I turned to walk away,

Why Me

they became violent and started lashing out at me. I managed to get loose, and as I backed away, one of them said, "If we ever see you again, serious harm will come to you because all the other boys will be here also."

I experienced various incidents like this one during my growing. Some were not as dramatic, and some were even more frightening. Somehow I kept arriving in awkward situations and had to keep finding diplomatic ways to back track so I wouldn't cause further trouble for myself. As I grew, I learned to be cautious, to isolate myself, and to choose my company and even my dialogue very carefully.

As I sat reminiscing in my mind as a boy, I realised I was, a strange boy from a broken home. I had started with nothing and created material wealth beyond my wildest dreams. I had dodged harm many times and fulfilled all my wildest dreams, or so I thought at the time. But inside I felt a little bitter and deprived from the so-called norm—the lifestyle I watched others have.

I worked every day, rising early to train my weedy body. Then I'd head off for my day job. I had a part-time entrepreneurial endeavor as well. Every Saturday, I'd visit the wholesale factories in the East End and pick up samples of boots and articles of clothing. I'd take these around to various shops and cafes and take orders. I'd fill the orders and pick up new samples the following Saturday, and during my tea breaks and lunch breaks, I'd make deliveries. At the end of my working day, I would return home, eat, and then head off to work as a security guard seven nights a week. Life was hard because I did nothing but work. As I watched and heard friends and others enjoying the socializing at the weekends and booking holidays, I didn't think at the time that I was losing out. Yes, they were all having fun, but it was my choice not to give myself any down time. I had one focus: make a lot of money, save my money, and start a business. This, I felt, would enable me to do all the things others were doing.

What I didn't realize was that time waits for no man. My work regime never stopped. Well, it finally did stop when I was completely worn out and extremely unwell. So I did feel a little bitter and almost pitied myself because I didn't have the ability and intelligence to know too much of anything. So I began to focus on the good I had in my life that was left, and in turn that forced me examine the not so good. Some of the negative aspects were commitments with people who weren't loving. Perhaps they just didn't have my best interests at heart, and I couldn't have had their interests at heart because of the state I was in. That's when I started to see whom I really loved and wanted to be with. And I recognized those who were just around for their own ride. So not only had I lost many material things, I had started to lose faith in people, even close family members.

If you're in a hot air balloon and you're not making progress, you must dump ballast over the side. The initial move toward freedom is to let go of what keeps you grounded in fear and worry. After you dump the first negative part of your life, you feel lighter. And with each successive thing you dump, in an extraordinary way you start to feel free. You believe you may be able to live and fly again.

Letting go of the first possession or person was the hardest for me. After that, it became almost beautiful to feel release and freedom.

When I received my life mediumship qualification on my last day with my teacher, I felt as though I had achieved something that was going to take me places I thought I had already been. But this time I would go there with balance, with love, and without greed, fear, suffering, or pain. I had thought I had qualified with many things in my life, but somehow I now had a real purpose. And my purpose was not to acquire or desire; rather, it was to be able to do something that put faith and hope in every single soul I came across. After researching and studying many subjects in my life, this, I discovered, was what I wanted most—to be able to help. I did not want to buy people cars or help them develop successful businesses or even save them from their own stress. I wanted to help them create by helping and guiding them as best I could, so they would know that they could start their new beginning. Somehow, everything seemed to make sense—not only where I was going, but also where I belonged.

Chapter 20

Like a Duck to Water

During my intensive six-month mediumship course, my teacher brought in random people—sitters they are called. These were people whom mediums could connect with their loved ones who had passed. I thought they were just everyday people. As they sat for me, I tried to perfect and deliver the gift I'd been born with. I felt like a duck taking to water. After every reading, the sitters would give feedback forms to my tutor, and we would critique my progress. This was very different from my life-long relationship with mediumship, which had consisted merely of randomly passing messages along to people when they came to me.

After I finished my course, my tutor said, "Now go out and search. Sit with as many mediums and clairvoyants as you can and see how others deliver their gift." So that is what I did. Much to my surprise, some were incredible and some were ... well, not as good as I thought they should be. This was another learning

The Medium

opportunity for me because, as I sat before these people as a compete stranger, not exposing who I was or my intentions, I got a profound impression as to whether they really were what they said they were, especially if I could or couldn't see the spirits they were telling me were talking to me. If they were really there, I could see for myself and hear their messages and receive the medium's interpretation of what was being said.

After such sittings, I thought, *My, my! I can do this professionally!* And that gave me the confidence. I hadn't known how much faith my tutor had in me. His plan had been created many months earlier. Some of these sitters he had brought in for me, I learned later, were fellow mediums. Some were very successful spiritual people who ran highly successful events. They were there to test me.

My tutor asked me to contact a man. He said the man already knew me. He was one of the mediums my tutor had brought in during my training, knowing full well that, if I convinced him of my craft, he might some day give me give me an opportunity to work in the world of professional mediumship. At the time, he was fully booked with a list of mediums awaiting a slot at his events. Again, the spirits had set it up. One of this man's best mediums was retiring, and he offered me opportunity to take a place at one of his shows. Of course, I hastily accepted.

The day grew near. Never before had I been so scared of anything. I had achieved many things. I had lectured on business, motivation, and success. But I had done that after preparation and planning. I knew that, if I prepared to plan, I planned to succeed.

This time, with my gift of mediumship, there was no planning. There was no preparing; there were no props. I didn't even have something to hold as tarot readers do. It would be just me, another person, and hopefully a loved one that person had lost. As I sat that first day, I remembered my tutor telling me that the spirits would never let me down—ever. "I absolutely assure you," he'd said. So, if nothing else, I had abundant faith. I have to say it was incredible. For the first time in my life, I was doing something I truly loved. And I was also seeing the faces and feeling the energy of the beautiful people sitting before me along with their loved ones in spirit form. The messages were so diverse; it was as though, on many occasions, the pain lifted from my sitters as I passed messages to them. In turn, I felt lifted, knowing I had made a difference in somebody's life who may have been suffering because he or she needed answers and reassurance.

Within a year, I had started to build a reputation, this time not of a good builder or businessman, but now one of a person who, through his special gift, could really help heal other people. Never had I ever felt such worth and appreciation, let alone love. Before long I realized this was my path and would remain so until my final departing. Nothing else could bring such joy into my life and into others' lives.

As I reported back to my tutor about my progress, he responded with a bombshell, saying he had known this was my path. However, he believed that, if I did nothing but practice my mediumship, I might become detached from reality, and that wouldn't be good for my soul and my grounding. I was adamant that I would not return to the daily race that had swallowed me whole. After much discussion and deliberating with my tutor, one day I asked my spirit guide, "What shall I do? I am being told—and I agree—that I must pursue an additional path so my new purpose doesn't become harmed." My guide quickly told me to use my life's adventures and skills and failures to help others with inspirational addresses: "Present your journey. Others may recognize themselves in your story, and you can help them to be free so they can achieve all they desire.

The next day I rang my tutor. After we talked for an hour or so, he said exactly the same thing. I had thought my whole life that one day I would write everything down for others to read. I hoped all my challenges might help them find their own way through their challenges.

I started writing about various parts of my life; however, the story was too vast. How could I put fifty years in a few hundred pages? My tutor advised to begin with the beginning. That would be the first book. I should just write what came to me, what flowed.

So one quiet day, I sat, pen ready in hand. I paused and drew a blank. You have to remember I was never an academic, let alone a writer. I hadn't written more than a page in thirty years. Could I really begin the first book of my life and make it not only interesting, but helpful and inspiring to others?

As I put the tip of the pen on the first page, the words came to me. Whether they were right or wrong or in the right place, thoughts just flowed and didn't stop. Hour after hour, tear after tear, I wrote my life story. I relived so many incidents. Some of it hurt, but most of it helped me to be true now, to heal old wounds, to put to rest what had been buried in my personal basement.

My concern then was that I was just covering the tip of the iceberg. Would an overview be enough? How much healing and letting go must I yet do if I was to continue resurrecting and opening up my life? It was then that the penny dropped: Life is a journey not a destination, and even if I was the only person in the whole world who would read what I had written, that would heal me, and that feeling would take me to a greater place of personal development.

With that compelling thought, I continued. I didn't know where it would take me, just as we don't know where life will take us, I suppose. We do what we can, do our best, but never truly know what we're going to get. As I created the journey of my life so far on paper I realized I'd never get it all in one book, so I continued with the intention to create a beginning, and if it helped me as well as others, then I'd have a base to continue. I would be able to write other books that would document my progress as my life evolved.

So, here I am, a full-time medium who has a desire to one day use my life's trials and tribulation and calamities for good, to help others find in themselves their purpose and confidence in the knowledge that the future can be bright, no matter what you've gone through. Each and every experience and chapter is about learning.

Why Me

It's easy to roll over and give up, and sadly, that's what many do when the wind is just about to change for them for the better. All will be well as long as we know in our hearts and souls that behind every cloud is sunshine, and if we walk toward the sun, shadows will always fall behind us. Knowing that, we can all hang on and keep trying with the belief that we are also watched and loved from far beyond our naked eye.

Chapter 21

Life as a Medium

Developing my life with spirits gives me hope. Some say mediums are born and psychics are made. If we hold that thought for a moment and assume that it is correct, that leaves possibilities for you far beyond anything you might have dreamed before you read this book.

Some may read the story here and disagree, I know I must respect that, but for those of you who would like to explore your hidden potential, I'll share some tell-tale signs and markers that you may want to consider and apply to your own life. So let me begin.

All people feel energy. Even babies feel it. I hope you also agree that we all are intrigued by what we can't see. Some of us squirm and turn away when we watch a scary film, or we cover our ears when someone is telling a story about the unknown. But we still want to watch and listen. And we question whether we believe all that "spooky" stuff or not. If we didn't believe or weren't intrigued, we wouldn't watch or listen. Well, the first step is to know that all people are psychic. From there you can decide to explore the phenomenon further in yourself. Or you could put it to rest and forget it for now. You could wait until you are ready to explore again. This usually will happen after a period in your life during which you need questions answered, but all your searching has given you no answers. At this point, you may allow desperation to lead you to think and explore beyond your normal levels and boundaries.

The first thing to remember is that, if we truly trust our feelings, which are usually right, we can make the right choices and decisions. It's when our feelings become contaminated by the voices and opinions of others along with our past experiences that the newly forming feelings can be taken over and further pressured or dismissed by the thoughts in our heads. Then we can find ourselves charging off in a direction far different from where we would be if we worked longer with our intuitive selves until everything became clear. Most people know in their hearts, in their guts, when feelings are right. They know when things will end up right, if they follow through. The outcome may be good or bad. Allow me to share with you how I learned to go with my gut and what it did for me when my mother and others forbade me from talking with spirits (and partly I agreed as, it at times, they scared and concerned me). I tapped into using my positive feelings and perceive knowing.

What I found was that, if I shared my intuitive feelings with others, I usually ended up in the wrong place. However, if I just closed my thoughts and my mouth, usually what I felt was going to happen happened—or it didn't happen if I thought it wouldn't. So, in time, I learned to trust my opinions until they became facts. In that way I could not be redirected to a different route by the opinions of others.

Here's an example. I had a strong feeling that buying a certain property was right for me in every way. I held onto those heartfelt gut feelings and kept my decision to myself. But then, before I made the purchase, I told other people about my decision. After they shared their negative thoughts, I had a hundred reasons not to go on my gut feeling.

Here's another example. Say I met a new person and felt quite good about him. Perhaps he had a kind heart and was sensitive. Our friendship could develop if I just stuck with my gut feeling, which is usually right. But then, if I asked others their opinions about that person, they might build a picture in my head based on their experience and feelings. So now I'd be preprogrammed to include others' opinions along with my own gut feelings. This could easily block the flow of energy I had been feeling and probably block the new person's ability to be his true self with me in an open-hearted, clean, clear way.

We must remember that no two humans communicate with each other in the same way. As I learned to really trust my intuitive feelings, I became assured that I could totally trust it. Then I realized it was totally real for me and I *must* trust it totally, even with my life. In that way I have survived and endured so many experiences, some of which could have cost me my life.

Once I accepted this completely, I felt great ease and peace and inner calm. Stupidly, however, at one point in my life or maybe two, I felt it so strongly that I didn't do a thing to drive myself forward, and in standing still, my intuition went to sleep, and I had to seek reassurance and guidance from others. Learning to trust one's self, knowing *what* is right not *who* is right, and then using all our learned behavior and skills to apply ourselves and achieve our desired outcome can, with patience, help us master our chosen paths and move forward on our ongoing journeys.

Chapter 22

Know Yourself

In order to have integrity ourselves and to encourage others to trust us, we must walk the talk. So, as I got to the last chapter of this book, I felt that a slowing down was required. I didn't know why, but I trusted my intuition and put my writing on hold. Until today, I hadn't written for three months, and I was right to do that because my intuition was right. During these three months, I've had to do battle with a carcinoma. I endured an operation to remove it, and I have survived. That's another chapter behind me and a new one to press on with. As it is said, we should remember the past, but we should not reside in it. However, we must learn from the past and revisit it as often as necessary to help us plot a better future.

Making my decisions according to my gut feeling has now become part of my everyday life. And it becomes more lovely with each day, for I can trust I am being guided, supported, loved, and cared for. Furthermore, I never feel alone, and even when challenges are cast upon me, I know they are for my benefit and learning experience, so I embrace them, knowing that, when I come out the other end, I will be better for them.

In order to start acknowledging our gut feeling, we need to start small. Let me show you how. We begin by finding our inner selves, and that happens when we learn to meditate quietly and listen and understand the source of our resonating breath. Once we are able to achieve this, we can elevate our focus and unlock the key to our inner being. This enables realization and knowing. What occurs around us affects what's within us. Thus, we receive a clear understating that whatever occurs in our lives, we are safe, knowing our inner selves are safe because nobody can unlock and enter our inner selves but ourselves. Once this is established and we trust in this fact implicitly, even an act of physical harm cannot penetrate our core and harm us. Also, once established, it will open automatically when necessary to warn, advise, guard and teach us to respond positively or negatively to give us the best possible outcome for our own well-being.

As you read this, you probably can recognize that some of what I've discussed has already happened to you. All that's necessary is to establish the connection and monopolize it, enhancing and improving it, for it is an ongoing process. It was for me, and after almost fifty years, I'm still trying to improve and enhance the process and make it as complete in mind, body, and spirit as humanly possible. The key is to realize it's not an inner voice like the voice we all have talking to us all the time. It comes first as feelings. Then our inner voices explain to us what we should, or perhaps shouldn't, do. I assure you, once you understand this and are able to listen to your instincts, they will never, ever, ever let you down, not matter what.

As I look back at every single thing that has happened in my life, I know I could have changed for the better or worse if only I had been conscious of this inner feeling and had connected it, stepped back, assessed it, and established that I should follow through by acting, delaying, or stopping all together. My only regret is that I wish I knew a long time ago what I know now. I think that's the same for a lot of people. I sincerely hope that, in reading my story, maybe you will adopt some of my ideas. It if nothing else, please know that your abilities are endless, and you really can achieve and survive anything life throws at you.

If you remain humble—or like me, learn to become humble—eradicate your ego, trust in yourself, believe your boundaries are endless and the possibilities to create a world for yourself and those you love can be achieved, then the only person stopping you is you. Forgive yourself first. The past is a ceremony of which you may only look back at when you have passed over. Now is your time to create a world. Start from the inside out, from the feelings you have inside, and in turn you will survive. In any real-world calamity or trauma, you will be guided by your inner psychic voice, a voice that every single one of us holds but only a few choose to acknowledge and access. Is really ours to hold onto for life.

May your journey be as pure as your thoughts and as beautiful as you are, for if nothing else, you know anything is possible because you are truly gifted. If you tap into and unleash your gift, it can provide you a life you perhaps have only dreamed of having.

Chapter 23

Older and Wiser

As I grew from a child into a man, I was told as I got older that time would move much faster, accelerating year by year, and eventually decade by decade. So, as this was what I was expecting, I watched out for it, and it did happen at times through my half century on this earth. But also I noticed, at times, that time would slow down and almost seem to stop.

I can only explain it like this: In the past, when I was troubled or lost or didn't know what to do, I would do nothing—literally nothing. I would just sit and wait. Even my mind would somehow stop thinking. It was as if I was suspended in animation. I would just do the usual daily life things like wash, eat, sleep, and exchange pleasantries with people, until something inside me triggered action, and I would be like a man on a mission.

Here's an example. All of a sudden, I got a bee in my bonnet about learning how to keep fish. So I was off to the library to become an expert on fish and their care. I visited tropical fish shops and aquariums. I talked fish until I had exhausted every area I could on the subject. Then, once I had mastered the subject to my own desired standards, I moved on to something else. Now, my parents accused me of being a five-minute wonder boy. What they didn't understand was that I was preparing myself to be an entrepreneur. You see, an entrepreneur needs many skills, not just experience in one industry. He also needs to be able to sit and do nothing as time passes, awaiting his next project or acquisition. So I was so misunderstood by so many. Some even questioned my ability and even wondered if I ever would equate to anything, as I seemed to just be jumping from one endeavor to another. "Big ideas!" Dad said sarcastically, bless him.

My hidden agenda, however, wasn't my competent thinking; it was my mediumship ability and all that came with it. It transitioned on from learning about fish keeping or mastering a martial art or becoming an ornithologist to running multiple businesses. What I soon came to realize was that I wasn't running my life; it was running me, and I didn't know how or when to stop because I didn't know what the stopping point looked or felt like. I just kept on going for dear life, propelled by the inertia of being lost in the thick of complications.

I was drowning in a complicated personal life, a complicated business life, a complicated family life and so on, with no understanding of how it would end or how to end it. My only way out was to become unwell. Now I believe that the breakdown of my body was the best possible thing that could have happened to me, for I am here to write my story and have a second chance at life.

I think thus far I have been one of the fortunate ones to be given this second chance. My gratitude for this position humbles me to my core. I wish with all sincerity that any person reading this will be given the chance as I was if at all necessary, to complete their journey in a way that gives them inner peace and personal satisfaction.